Generosity

BY CYNTHIA AMOROSO

Published by The Child's World®
1980 Lookout Drive • Mankato, MN 56003-1705
800-599-READ • www.childsworld.com

Acknowledgments
The Child's World®: Mary Berendes, Publishing Director
The Design Lab: Design
Pamela J. Mitsakos: Photo Research
Christine Florie: Editing

Photographs ©: David M. Budd Photography: 5, 9, 11; iStockphoto.com/ChristopherBernard: 19; iStockphoto.com/DistinctiveImages: 17; iStockphoto.com/Kali Nine LLC: 7; iStockphoto.com/Perkmeup Imagery: 15; iStockphoto.com/Sharon Dominick: 13; iStockphoto.com/skynesher: cover, 1; iStockphoto.com/Steve Debenport Imagery: 21

ISBN 9781623235192
LCCN 2013931448

Printed in the United States of America
Mankato, MN
July, 2013
PA02172

ABOUT THE AUTHOR

Cynthia Amoroso is Director of Curriculum and Instruction for a school district in Minnesota. She enjoys reading, writing, gardening, traveling, and spending time with friends and family.

Table of Contents

What Is Generosity?

Generosity is giving to others without expecting something in return. When you are generous, you want to help others. You are not thinking of yourself. You give because you want others to feel good.

Generosity is a way of being kind to others.

Generosity with Time

You have had a busy day at school. You have a lot to think about. You have a lot to do. Then you notice that your friend is sad. You are really busy! But you still take time to talk to him. You ask him if you can help. You show generosity by taking time to listen.

Sharing some time with people can really help them out.

Generosity with Food

You have brought cookies in your lunch box. Your friend sits next to you. He does not have any cookies. The cookies you brought are your **favorite** kind. You would like to eat them all! But you know your friend likes them, too. You show generosity by sharing your cookies with him.

Sometimes generosity means giving away things we like.

Generosity with Your Things

You love to draw with markers. You have lots of markers in different colors. Other kids in your class do not have as many as you do. You show generosity by sharing your markers. Now you can all have a better time drawing!

It feels good to share what you have.

Generosity with Money

You have been saving your money to buy a new toy. You cannot wait to get it! Then you learn in school about children in need. They do not have money for warm clothes. They do not have enough food. You would like to help them. You show generosity by **donating** some of your money.

You can show generosity by sharing money with people in need.

Generosity with Your Knowledge

Are you really good at something? Maybe you can sing. Maybe you know how to dance or draw. Or maybe you read really well. You can show generosity by sharing your knowledge. You can help somebody else learn these things. Teaching a younger kid can be fun! And it can make a big difference.

Helping others learn is a way to show generosity.

Generosity at Home

There are many ways to show generosity at home. You might not like your sister's favorite TV show. You can let your sister watch it anyway. Maybe feeding the dog is not your job. You can feed the dog anyway. Showing generosity is not just for friends and classmates. It is for family, too!

Being generous to your family is nice!

Generosity with Feelings

Maybe some people seem different from you. Maybe they do or say things you do not like. It might be easy to be mean to them. You could get upset. You could say, "I do not like you." But you show generosity instead. You try to understand their side. You give them a fair chance.

Generosity means not being too hard on people.

Generosity Makes a Difference!

Showing generosity means sharing with others. Sharing with people can really help them out. It makes their lives better. It makes your life better, too. How can you show generosity today?

Generosity makes the world a better place!

Glossary

donating–Donating something is giving it away, often to people in need.

favorite–When you like something best, it is your favorite.

Learn More

Books

Chamberlin, Mary. *Mama Panya's Pancakes.* Cambridge, MA: Barefoot Books, 2005.

Chinn, Karen. *Sam and the Lucky Money.* New York: Lee & Low Books, 1995.

Fleming, Candace. *Boxes for Katje.* New York: Farrar, Straus and Giroux, 2003.

Web Sites

Visit our Web site for links about generosity: **childsworld.com/links**

Note to Parents, Teachers, and Librarians: We routinely verify our Web links to make sure they are safe and active sites. So encourage your readers to check them out!

Index